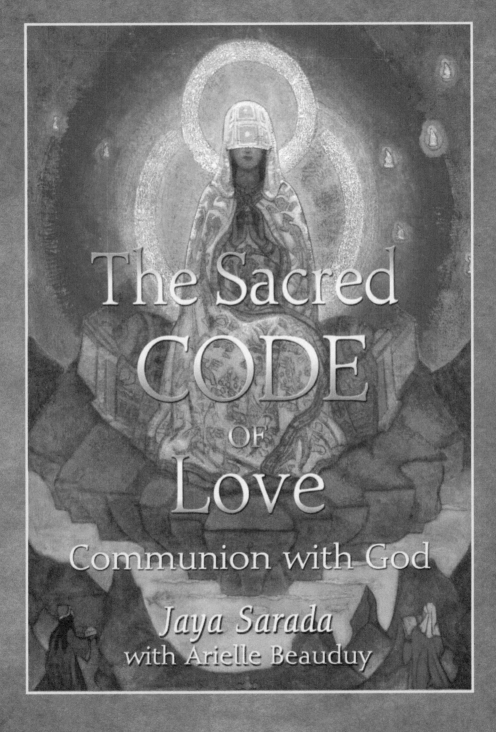

The Sacred
CODE
OF
Love

Communion with God

Jaya Sarada
with Arielle Beauduy

Jewels of Light Publishing

14300 NE 20th Avenue D-102 #383

Vancouver, WA 98686

1.855.50 JEWEL (505.3935)

JewelsofLight.com

Cover Art "Mother of the World"

Back Cover Art "Madonna Oriflamma"

Courtesy of Nicholas Roerich Museum, www.roerich.org

ISBN: 978-1-893037-12-0

The Sacred Code of Love
Communion with God

Cover & Interior Design by: Dianne Rux - DzinerGraphics.com

Thank You

Cover and Interior Photo Credits:

"The Mother of the World" sketch, Banners of the East series, 1924, front cover art, and "Madonna Oriflamma," Tempera on canvas, 1932, back cover art, Courtesy of the Nicholas Roerich Museum, www.roerich.org

Arielle Beauduy – Hawaii Photographs
Jaya Sarada – Ojai, California; Shasta, California; Sedona, Arizona; Big Sur, California; Vedanta Temple of Santa Barbara, California; Meditation Mount in Ojai, California; Krotona Institute of Theosophy in Ojai, California; New Camaldoli Hermitage in Big Sur, California. California and Oregon Coast, Rivers of Oregon, Washington Gorge, Portland Rose Garden, Japanese Garden of Portland, Krishnamurti Oak Grove Ojai, California; Self-Realization Fellowship Lake Shrine Temple in Pacific Palisades, California

Nina Kirby – Shasta, California Pictures, www.crystalclan.com

Robert Glenn – Roses and Flowers, www.robertglennphotography.com

"If the only prayer you said in your whole life was, "Thank you," that would suffice."
Meister Eckhart

Blessings & Gratitude

Deep gratitude to the wonderful people who assisted in birthing

The Sacred Code of Love

I give my heartfelt gratitude to my daughter Arielle Beauduy for being instrumental in creating this book. As the translator and editor of the messages, her writing not only conveys the truth of them, but she also invites the reader on a profound journey into *The Sacred Code of Love.* Her presence creates an atmosphere of Divine light and love in which to receive the messages of Jeshua and Miriam.

To Patricia Frances, for her lifetime of love and friendship: thank you for your assistance in birthing *The Sacred Code of Love.*

To Dianne Rux, my friend, graphic artist, and book designer whose awesome work in all of the Jewels of Light creations has been an invaluable source of wisdom: I especially thank you for your loving attention in designing *The Sacred Code of Love*—a work of art!

Special thanks to Melanie Hornsby for her meticulous editing. We are so honored to have you on our team!

To Thomas Clarke, whose undying support has graced my life so that I may receive these messages and offer them to the world: you are eternally loved!

Agape:

A love filled with the joy of each other and the world;
the purest form of spiritual expression.
A Sacred Embrace.

Contents

May our hearts be pure.
May our deeds be good.
May our minds be at peace.
This is the way of God.
The way of the Sacred Code of Love.

Miriam of Magdela

Message to Beloved Readers

In life, most of us find ourselves oppressed by the world's conditioning, which insists that we become something different than we are. We allow ourselves to be molded by the world's standards. Living through authority, family lineage, and poor self-image are the roots of deep suffering.

Therefore, at some point, the question is asked, *"Who am I?"* This question leads to further inquiry such as, *"Who am I without my name, my status, my ancestry?"*

Reading this book or listening to the CD is an invitation to journey deeper into the truth of being and to encounter the Sacred energy that is the underlying force of all creation. Through stillness, this true and unconditional loving force appears in your life. It is Sacred energy that moves mountains to guide you on the path of return to your Divine being.

The passages in **The Sacred Code of Love** is the Divine guidance for your life, the work of Jeshua and Miriam and The Sacred Council of Light. It is a teaching on how to liberate your soul from the bondage of fear and conditioning. In reading these passages, you will gain insights into the truth of being, and you will receive a direct transmission of light from the Masters. And through such light, you will return to being a child of God, opening your heart to a greater love.

In your heart is a temple that holds the key to **The Sacred Code of Love**. The Sacred Council of Light will illuminate the path to your inner temple, so you may embrace the gifts of your eternal wellspring.

The Sacred Code of Love
is the way of Grace.

The Passage Through The Sacred Heart

Deep within our being there is a vast space of radiant presence known as the Sacred heart, the embodiment of unified God consciousness. This presence is the energetic form of a luminous lotus flower, which is connected to the lower area of our Heart Chakra (Anahata), within our Sushumna Channel (energetic channel around the spinal column). This spiritual energy is inscribed in the Upanishads, Vedic texts which date back to 6th or 7th BCE. Yogis and spiritual beings throughout history have tapped into the capacity of this energy, which holds a deep healing and mystical power.

Inside the lotus of our Sacred heart, which in Sanskrit is the Ananda Kanda lotus or "Space of Bliss," lives the "Celestial Wish Fulfilling Tree." The deepest yearning of our soul's potential of expression is held within this mystical tree, which thrives within the Ananda Kanda lotus. When we enter this magical energetic space of the Sacred heart, we feel the eternal joy of our true nature pouring into every cell of our being. This mysterious field, has never been affected or damaged, it remains pure and timeless throughout all of our life experiences.

The door to this boundless abiding space, opens through the devotion to our eternal true nature, through a blessed love, which naturally dissolves false identification with our internal or external world. Hridaya, a Sanskrit name for "he who dwells in the heart," is the seat of this awareness of our infinite unified being, our essential essence or true nature.

When we begin to turn toward unified God consciousness, the natural essence of devotion of our Sacred heart heals the discordant energy of our primitive human experience on the third dimensional plane of existence. The third dimensional plane, holds immense unnecessary suffering because it is bound in perceived psychology concepts of time and separation.

Through our souls' calling for **Communion with God**, we commence our courtship with the Divine. This love affair is what many spiritual poets write about; Hafiz, Kahlil Gibran, Rumi, and others throughout history. Through stillness, spiritual practices and expression, we initiate our transcendence of the third dimensional plane, and we enter the space known as the "dweller on the threshold." At this point, the human heart may break, and we may experience what is known as the "dark night of the soul," which is simply the dissolution of the known realm of the third dimension, our ancestral patterns, subconscious and conscious beliefs. The familiar, perceived suffering of life in time, disintegrates. This experience can be difficult because of the power of false negative beliefs that are released from the body, mind, Spirit trinity, and the feeling that one has been forsaken by God. But, this is a simple final misperception of the mind. The unchanging reality is that God consciousness is us, and so therefore we cannot be separate. This process can take a moment, or it can take a lifetime. Unfortunately, many never experience this at all.

Once we awaken through the direct experience of our eternal true essence, the grace of unified God consciousness fully takes over our being and life, and we transcend the sleeping realm of the third dimensions. Our essence then bridges with our Sacred heart as we step into the Unknown, the field of miracles. Our vibration is realized as the very breath of God itself in us, as us; which is the embodiment of the fifth dimension, and the complete opening of our Sacred heart, Anahata, "the unstruck space." In our marriage with God our life becomes the being of Holy service, the experience and offering of harmony, awareness, equilibrium, love, joy, light and grace. Every cell of our essence, is the reflection of our unity with God, permeating Mother Gaia and the Universe. Separation dissolves, in the totality of the realization of God, within and without.

The practice of *The Flowering of the Sacred Heart; Prayer, Presence, Release, Transcendence and Rest,* is an offering of compassionate guidance through the passageway of the Sacred heart, which brings the grace of the *Divine Trinity of Light, Wisdom and Love.*

We invite you to take a moment each day to experience *The Flowering of the Sacred Heart, A Devotional Practice of Communion with God.*

A Devotional Practice: Communion with God
The Flowering of The Sacred Heart

Prayer
Intention of God

Turn your attention inward with your palms placed softly on your heart. Sense the radiant presence of your being flood with breath of the Divine. Allow any thoughts of self to dissolve with your intention of unified God consciousness. Feel every cell of your being as a vibrational Holy temple of light.

The Intention of God allows what is false to simply drop away, and what is revealed is the presence of the unified God consciousness within you.

Presence
Witness of Being

Breathe in fully, bringing in fresh energy into every cell of your being. Breathe out, allowing the ease of presence to enter. Use your breath to bring your body, mind, and Spirit into the present. As your being settles fully in the now, begin to observe the transitory nature of all things, within and without. Feel the peace of your radiant presence as your true abiding, formless, and eternal nature. See that everything rooted in the mind; concepts, emotions, projections, assumptions, subjections, knowledge and memories, are all transitory, changeable, and limited in time. Witness how that which changes, will eventually cease, to exist and therefore has always been an illusion. These illusions, created by the mind, are not bad or good, but they can be useful in the realm of human life to fulfill desires. Suffering comes when there is a belief that the illusion is who you are. That which Is unified God consciousness does not change. It is formless and timeless.

In *Presence*, You are That which Is.

Release
Breathing Out, Altar of Surrender

Breathe out entirely, letting go of all things within and without. Place any discordant energy, power struggles, beliefs, or patterns of limitation on the altar of your Sacred heart. Allow pain and suffering to simply fall away with every breath of release. Your breath is the breath of Spirit, and in this Holy exchange with life, all is healed, and all is well. This moment, here and now, is full of abiding peace, despite all changes in the internal or external world. Turn inward to surrender to your Divine Source. See in this moment now that you are truly void of all the accumulation of suffering that you have perceived your precious heart holds. Through your breath, sense that the energetic lotus of your Sacred heart is flooded with the light of Holy truth.

Your *Release* is the beginning of Communion with God.

Transcendence
Breathing In, Receive God's Light and Love

On your breath in, feel you entire being awaken. Connect to the Source of who you are, your vitality center. This very act of connection rebirths your body, mind, and Spirit. Through your in-breath of Divine Spirit, you activate the lotus of your Sacred heart, and all your prayers are answered in the truth of your highest potential. God's light and love pours forth through every cell of your being and every cell of the universe. There is nothing more to gain and nothing to lose.

The *Transcendence* of that which if false, is the opening of your Sacred Heart.

Rest
The Grace of Unified God Consciousness.

Simply rest in grace.
The actualization, the embodiment of **_The Sacred Heart_ of God.**

The completion of Communion with God

Unlocking The Sacred Code of Love

The Sacred Code of Love is an invitation to open the door to your soul's highest expression. The activation of **The Sacred Code** within your heart will occur through daily study of these passages and the practice of the meditations. Each passage in *The Sacred Code of Love* has a Divine attribute that will be transmitted to you through reading, meditating, and repeating daily. Prior to reading each section, you are offered meditations to practice. Sit, at ease, in silence, to receive these passages. This time is important to receive the truth of these messages and to experience Sacred Love.

INVOCATION

"Together, We stand at the doorway to the Kingdom. The Holy Temple invites you to enter to receive the blessings of Jeshua, Miriam, and the Council of Light. We Are Sacred Love. We have been with you since the beginning of time and are here to help you awaken the Holy Presence within you. Your lifetime is ultimately for the realization of your Divinity. The awareness of the eternal, untouched God Consciousness within you will bring the tremendous blessings of our infinite Sacred Love, Light, Wisdom, and Joy. We are with you eternally, through the darkness and the Light. Within the stillness of your Sacred Heart, you will find our embrace. Take time each day to pray, and we will forever be by your side. Trust in Our Light, for you will soon realize it is your Light. Now, begin your Holy journey back to God."

We Are Sacred Love.

Jeshua and Miriam

Section Summary

1. **Sacred Love:** Sacred Love is a love that is unconditional in its expression. It holds the principles of Divine love, awakened in your heart.

2. **Unity:** Living in Unity means to be free of separation from your Divine Source. Unity is the integration of your inner being with God consciousness.

3. **Holy Medicine:** Holy Medicine is the will of God operating in your life, assisting you to reach your Divine potential.

4. **Genesis:** Genesis is your entry into your true Divine being. In the beginning, you were created from light, and you are always returning to this light.

5. **Stillness:** In Stillness, the Holy presence awakens in your Sacred heart, and in your Sacred heart, you hear the voice of Stillness.

6. **Remembering:** Remembering is freedom from mistaken identity. The time is now to remember your essential true nature.

7. **Awakening:** Awakening your inner true nature is the path to happiness. *The Sacred Code of Love,* when activated in your heart, is the key to your awakening.

8. **Light:** Light is the life force of Spirit; it is awakened in your Sacred Heart through returning to your Divine Source.

9. **Wellspring:** Within your Sacred heart flows an inexhaustible Wellspring of love and light. This eternally flowing Source will carry you to your Divine Home.

10. **The Gift of Seeing:** The Gift of Seeing is the way of the heart. The most precious gift to give another is to see their Divine nature.

11. **Master's Grace:** The Grace of the Master has awakened in your heart when the self surrenders to its Source.

"I stood upon a high mountain and saw a tall man,
and another of short stature,
and heard something like the sound of thunder
and went nearer in order to hear.
Then he spoke to me and said:
I am thou and thou art I,
and wherever thou art, there am I, and I am
sown in all things; and whence thou wilt,
thou gatherest me, but, when thou
gatherest me, then gatherest thou thyself.
I am the Light that illuminates all things.
I am All: from me all came forth,
and to me all is attained.
Split a piece of wood; I am there.
Lift up the stone, and you will find me there."

"The Kingdom of God is within you."

Gospel of Eve

Seek the truth in your life,
and the truth will tell you the story of creation.
Be authentic in your life, and your true nature
will light your path home.
Holy wisdom is the gift of your Divine being;
by seeking the Source of God within,
you open your heart to great joy.

"Teacher, which is the great commandment in the law?"
Jeshua said to him,
"You shall love the Lord your God
with all your heart, and with all your soul,
and with all your mind.
This is the great and first commandment.
And a second is like it,
You shall love your neighbor as yourself."

Luke 10:27

Sacred Love

The Light is Master's Grace in your heart.

Miriam of Magdala

Opening Your Sacred Heart

Take time each day to listen to your Sacred heart.
See that it is your personal temple where you
journey to let go of the sorrow of life.
It is through the practice of the Sacred heart that you
will come to know grace.
Healing is the work of the Sacred heart.
Open your Sacred heart to your Divine Source,
and let go of all that is no longer serving you.
In your surrender, the truth of your being emerges.

"Meditation is not a means to an end,
there is no end, no arrival;
it is a moment in time and out of time."
J. Krishnamurti

Take a moment to listen within your Sacred heart,
to feel what is there. In your heart lives the story of your life.
You are invited to surrender your story to the
Divine presence within your Sacred heart.
Breathing in, you reconnect with your true essence.
Breathing out, you let go of your life story.
Now, journey deeper into the temple of your Sacred heart.
There, you will leave the world and enter
the formless, eternal void.
This is your inner sanctuary
where you listen to the voice of God.

Sacred love is the doorway
to your heavenly realm of being.
You are now being guided
to enter the depth of your heart
so you may receive the light of the Divine.

The Sacred Code of Love is within you.
It is activated through communion
with your Divine Source.
When the Sacred Code of the heart is awakened,
the self may be realized.

Sacred love is the essence of your Divine being.
Within your heart lies a unity with all life,
your connection to God.

To light the fire of the heart, there must be yearning.
To awaken the wisdom of the heart,
there must be understanding.
The Sacred love of the heart is uncovered
by meditating on the Divine nature of life.

In this moment, see what is here now.
Invite the mind to dissolve into the heart.
Ask that your fear transform into
love, your birthright.
The Sacred Code of Love is the deliverance of fear
onto the altar of love in every Holy moment.

Your yearning for truth
will transcend the
manifested world;
you will enter the
mystical, unchanging, and
formless nature of life.

Light, Wisdom, and Love
are the principles of the Divine trinity.
The balance of these three qualities is
the foundation for your inner awakening.

"God is Love, and they that dwell in Love,
dwell in God, and God in them."

John 4:16

Time holds the possibility of realizing
your infinite connection to Source.
The eternal reality is the
background of time.
Turn toward that which is never changing,
and there, you will find your Divine being.

Grace is with you
throughout your life.
Sacred love uncovers
what has always
been present.

Sacred love is a path of devotion to Spirit.
It is the simple turning of attention
inward to the stream of Divine being.
The grace of Spirit then awakens in your life,
and true service begins.

In my heart lies the key to Sacred Love.

Meditate on the light of being and Sacred love.
The opening to heaven is through the
Divine heart, the way of grace.

Sacred love
is the universal force
behind all manifestation.
Within the physical world
lies the key
to awakening.

I Am
in Unity with the Divine.

Sacred love is
unity with the Divine.
Spirit is the groom,
and the soul is the bride.
Holy medicine is
the integration of the
Spirit and the soul,
a blessed marriage.

To love God with all your heart is the seed of Sacred love.
This love comes from deep longing
to reunite with your Divine Source.
Welcome this longing,
as it is the grace that opens your heart.

The life force is rejuvenated through
the awakening of spiritual light.
Healing occurs when the soul
remembers its true nature.

The truth of your being is that
you are an embodiment of the Divine.
Sacred love is the force
of this realization.

I Am Sacred Love.

Sacred love is knowing
you are nothing in the world of manifestation,
and yet, you are One with all creation.
This is the beauty of Divine being.

Sacred love will reveal
the truth of your Being.
Fear will hide the truth.
The more you love,
the more fear has no
place inside you.

Be open to God's love,
an embrace that surrounds
you, in every moment of
your precious journey.
Life will be difficult at times,
but the Divine will hold
your hand through the
valleys of sorrow
and the mountains of joy.

Life is so very precious.
In your heart lives the key to Sacred love.
In your mind resides the key to the light of the Divine.
Through your breath, you receive the gift of God.

Your Sacred practice begins by
releasing your mistaken identity.
You are filled with light in
this freedom, and you are
unified with the Divine.

Sacred love is the flame in the heart that
awakens in the student of Divinity.
Through surrender, this flame
dissolves all sense of separation from
your Divine Source and uncovers your eternal being.

Live in the light
of your heart,
rest in the love
of your heart,
and you will
know God.

"When you make the two into one,
and make the inner as the outer,
and the upper as the lower,
and make male and female into a single one,
so that the male shall not be male,
and the female shall not be female:
then you will enter the Kingdom of One."

Gospel of Thomas

Unity

Remember who you are in this most difficult life.
In remembering your True Nature,
life becomes One with the Divine.

Miriam of Magdala

Rest in Oneness

Your Sacred heart is the home
in which you will find the peace needed
to unify the fragmented parts of yourself.
In times of disturbance,
turn your mind to the Source of life itself,
and allow the love of your heart to heal all affliction.
Rest now in the consciousness of Oneness,
the place within yourself that is
surrendered to the peace of life.

"Still your mind in me, still yourself in me,
and without a doubt you shall be unified with me,
Lord of Love, dwelling in your heart."

Bhagavad Gita

Breathing in, turn your attention inward,
and drop into the temple of your Sacred heart.
Breathing out, empty your mind of thoughts, worries,
and concerns. Take a few more breaths, allowing yourself
to sink into a deeper peace.
Rest in the Oneness of your true and unchanging nature.
It is this rest that revitalizes your light being
and infuses your heart with Divine love.

The being who recedes back to its original
state of emptiness becomes unified with God.

I Am
in Union with my Divine Source.

A Holy life is the
integration of light and dark,
which is discovered in the silence of being.

The journey to your true home
is paved with the light of the Divine.
It begins with the surrender of the self
that is lost in worldly consciousness.

Sacred love is unity with all of creation.
Remember who you are on the journey
to the Kingdom of the Divine.

I Am
One with All of Life.

Both soul and body are Sacred vehicles
to return to your Divine home.
The physical body is the life force,
and the soul is the light body.
Together, you have a means to ascend
into a higher plane of consciousness,
where you meet your true self.

God is your Source of life.
A stream of Divine light flows through your heart,
and it is connected to the heart of God.
The purpose of life is to strengthen this stream
of Sacred connection with your Source,
allowing the light to guide you home.

Trust in Divine love to release you from the
burden of separation from your Sacred Source.
In your surrender, you will uncover your
magnificent being.

The road to the highest plane
of consciousness
is through the heart of Divine love.

When the truth originates
in the heart, the
mind becomes
a vessel of light,
freed from conflict.
The mind is simply a
tool for life to function.
When you are
devoted to the
Sacred presence
within your heart,
you will surrender your
mind to this Holy force.

59

I Am Light. I Am Divine. I Am Love.

"The Consciousness in you,
and the Consciousness in Me,
apparently two, really One,
seek Unity and that is Love."

Nisargadatta Maharaj

The song of the Beloved is
calling you. Drift into the
melody of pure
consciousness, the
background
of all of creation.

Come to the altar of Sacred love,
and lay down your worldly burdens.
Receive your birthright of
beauty, joy, and freedom,
the essence of your Divine being.

In quietude, all accumulation dissolves,
revealing the light of the Spirit and the love of the soul.
The emptying of the self uncovers the purest state of being.

Sacred love is the
mystical heart in
Oneness with all of life.
It is an opening to your
Divine Source
and a release of self-affliction.

The invitation is to live a Sacred life in which
peace of being is your natural state.
In this consciousness, you rest in your true nature,
remaining at peace despite all outward changes.

Love is the natural expression of the self
in its child-like state of innocence.
Remember the purest wonder of your being,
free of thoughts lost in the sea of worldly consciousness.

You are the keeper of the flame of love.
You hold the key to its inherent grace.

Sacred love opens your
path to the Divine.
Remember the light is
always shining on your path,
the way of eternal joy
and freedom.

Life is a canvas in which the colors
of joy and sadness appear.
The background is your true and abiding nature,
which remains in its original state.
Open to the beginning, and you will know the end.

The light of the Divine is always with
you as you journey through life.
Ask and you shall receive the love
you need to overcome life's tests.

Holy wisdom is the light in your heart,
Sacred love is the grace in your heart.
In this awareness, you are One with the Divine.

"I was supremely happy, for I had seen.
Nothing could ever be the same.
I have drunk at the clear and pure waters,
and my thirst was appeased.
I have seen the Light.
I have touched compassion which
heals all sorrow and suffering;
it is not for myself, but for the world.
Love in all its glory has intoxicated my heart;
my heart can never be closed.
I have drunk at the fountain of joy and eternal beauty.
I am God-intoxicated."

J. Krishnamurti

Holy Medicine

Seek first the Kingdom of God,
and the Kingdom will become your Home.

Miriam of Magdala

Your True Essence

Death of the separate sense of self will reveal the
truth of your Being that has always been present.
Open to the truth now, as it is the Source of joy
and rejuvenation for your body, mind, and Spirit.
The past is the shackle of bondage that holds you
captive to the sorrow of mistaken identification.
God will assist you to die to the past and be reborn
to the light being of your true essence.

"The flowering of meditation is goodness,
and the generosity of the heart
is the beginning of meditation."

J. Krishnamurti

Open now to your radiant being of light.
See that your true essence has always been present
throughout all of your life's changes.
While you breathe in,
receive the light and love of the Divine.
While you breathe out,
let go of the sorrow of separation.
Seek the Source of your life,
and you will know Sacred love.

The breath of the Divine is breathing you.
Holy medicine is the Source
of all energy and life.
Trust that it will illuminate your path
and remove the darkness
of misidentification.

I Am
the Way of Truth and Light.

The Sacred light of Holy
medicine will transform the
human state of sorrow into the
Divine realm of perfection;
in this, you will find freedom of being.

Divine law is operating in your life
through the trials of awakening.
At times when rejuvenation is
needed, ask for assistance,
and you will be renewed in
body, mind, and Spirit.

Open your heart to your inner beauty,
the flowering of God within.

Holy medicine uncovers what has never been damaged—your soul.
The Source and truth of your being is whole.

Your heart contains an eternal wellspring of love
that is forever available to you.

The wisdom of Holy medicine is to surrender
to the truth of who you are.

In your deepest heart,
know yourself as the embodiment of the Divine.

Time is a gift from the Divine to reach your soul's potential.
Use this time wisely, for within these moments lives the
possibility of evolving love and grace.

"If the doors of perception were cleansed
everything would appear to man as it is, infinite."

William Blake

Holy medicine is the truth of your Divine being.
Through its light, healing
becomes a natural occurrence.

Teach love by living love in all expressions of your life.
When you surrender your smaller self into your greater self,
your magnificent being awakens.

The path of life is
the journey of
returning to your
essential true nature.
All experiences, whether
good or bad,
increase the heart's
capacity to hold more
love, truth, and light.

The road to your Divine nature is paved with
blessings of truth, joy, freedom, and Sacred love.
Take this precious life to remember who you are.

"In tribulation, immediately draw near to God
with confidence, and you will receive strength,
enlightenment, and instruction."

St. John of the Cross

Genesis

The Holy life is your birthright
as you enter the Kingdom of the Divine.

Miriam of Magdala

Seek First the Kingdom

Remember now that your life's purpose is
to return to your Divine home.
Each day, take a few moments to discover the riches
of the Kingdom, which are the gifts of life.
You will find these gifts within your Sacred heart
as you uncover what has always been held within.
The Kingdom is the place within
where the light shines in your sorrow.

"Meditation brings Wisdom,
lack of meditation leaves ignorance.
Know what leads you forward and what holds you back,
and choose the path the leads you to Wisdom."

Buddha

Breathing in, allow your mind to soften
within your Sacred heart.
Now, breathing out, let go of your mind,
of worldly concerns and worries,
while invoking the Divine to bring you to a greater peace.
Seek first the truth of your life, and the truth will set you free.
In your freedom, you will find yourself
in the Kingdom of God. This is your True home.

A new beginning is the gift from Spirit.
The invitation is to surrender the past,
to renew your innocent being
of freedom, light, and joy.

Begin now on your life
path of understanding.
Beyond the patterns of conditioning,
you will arrive at the
gateway of the Kingdom.

Inner seeing is when
you awaken
to the cause of sorrow.
The light is always shining
in all aspects of your life.
This Sacred light
will guide you
to the truth of being and
remove the roots of suffering.

"Lord, make me an
instrument of Your peace.
Where there is hatred,
let me sow love;
where there is injury, pardon;
where there is doubt, faith;
where there is despair, hope;
where there is darkness, light;
where there is sadness, joy.
O, Divine Master, grant that I
may not so much seek to be
consoled as to console; to be
understood as to understand;
to be loved as to love;
For it is in giving
that we receive;
it is in pardoning that
we are pardoned;
it is in dying that we are
born again to eternal life."

Saint Francis

Be true to yourself, and then you will be true to the Divine.
Love yourself, and you will love the Divine.
In this, you will dance in the beauty of God's creation.

"The moment you have in your heart,
this extraordinary thing called Love,
and feel the depth, the delight, the ecstasy of it,
you will discover that for you,
your world is transformed."

J. Krishnamurti

God, the universal consciousness of love and light,
is the Source of all, and you are born from this Source.
Remember your Sacred origin by
accepting your Divinity.

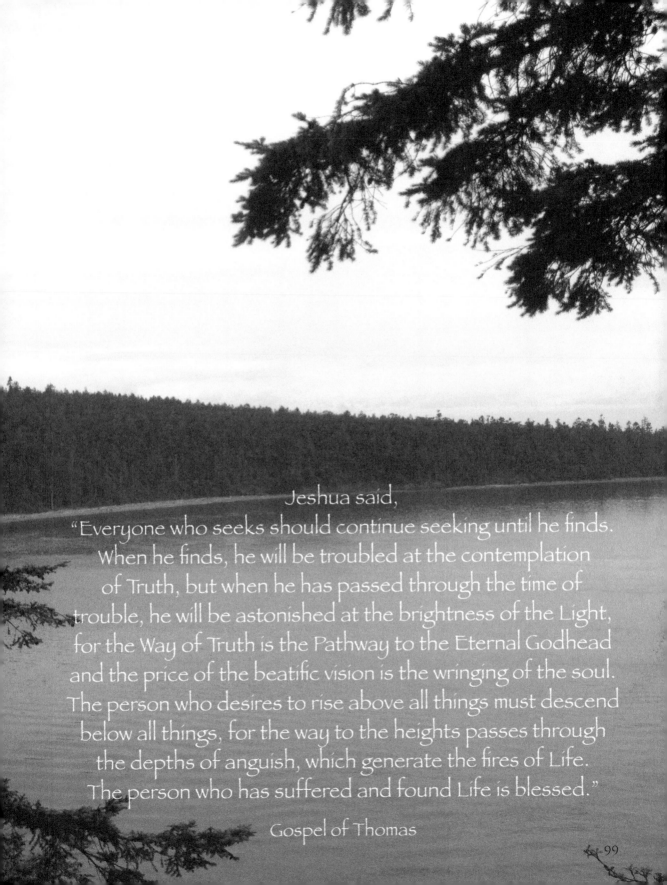

Jeshua said,
"Everyone who seeks should continue seeking until he finds.
When he finds, he will be troubled at the contemplation
of Truth, but when he has passed through the time of
trouble, he will be astonished at the brightness of the Light,
for the Way of Truth is the Pathway to the Eternal Godhead
and the price of the beatific vision is the wringing of the soul.
The person who desires to rise above all things must descend
below all things, for the way to the heights passes through
the depths of anguish, which generate the fires of Life.
The person who has suffered and found Life is blessed."

Gospel of Thomas

Today, the light of the Holy presence
is guiding your way.
Inside your heart, there is a temple of light
where we will meet.
This is the most Sacred communion.

Mary says, "Will the thirst for knowledge ever be quenched?"
Jeshua said,
"When once you have drunk from the spring of knowledge,
you will return again and again, for each
time your thirst is satisfied,
a new thirst will grow, greater than the first.
The more you drink, the greater will be your desire to drink,
but in the intensity of your desire, you will be filled.
I tell you the truth when I say that whoever seeks will find,
and the finding will cause him to seek,
but in the seeking is hidden the meaning of life."

Gospel of Thomas

"You are the Light of the world.
Let your Light so shine."

Mathew 5:16

The original essence of pure consciousness
is underlying all activity of the self.
In your true nature, you are
an eternal wellspring of Sacred love.

Jeshua speaks of the Kingdom:
"The Kingdom is inside of you,
and it is outside of you.
When you come to know yourselves,
then you will become known,
and you will realize that it is you
who are the sons of the living father.
But, if you will not know yourselves,
you dwell in poverty, and it is you
who are that poverty."

Gospel of Thomas

Stillness

The Sacred Code of Love is awakened
in your heart of innocence.

Miriam of Magdala

Letting Go

Take each day to let go of the accumulation of negative
thoughts and reactions to life's changing experiences.
Soon, you will see what is true never changes.
Forgetting the self is a practice of emptying thought;
what remains is pure consciousness.

"Playfully, you hid from me, all day I looked,
then I discovered I was you,
and the celebration of that began."

Lalla

Begin now by breathing deeply while visualizing yourself
under a beautiful, blue, crystal clear waterfall.
As the water touches your head, see it cleansing you
from the accumulated thought in your mind.
Feel the lightness of being without thought, and see your life
as being free from stress and worry about the future,
living fully in the now.

Become as still as a mountain, and
surrender to its majesty.
Live as though you were on top of the mountain,
seeing your life as the beauty of creation.

Time is a gift which allows you to travel
inward to the light of the Divine.
On this journey of life, you will be
beckoned to the Kingdom.
Open your being to hear the call of God.

Rest upon the altar of your heart.
Surrender the movements of your mind
to the vibrant emptiness within you.

The deepest
spiritual teachings are
discovered in your
Sacred heart.
The secret of God
is waiting for you.

Open the door to
your Sacred heart.
Step over the
threshold of resistance
and enter the
temple of awakening.
It is when you
renounce your separate
sense of self that
Divine grace
is bestowed upon you.

See now that you are purely a light being,
a soul without an identity, a brilliant energy
infinitely connected to Source.
This is a profound truth, as it liberates you
from the bondage of your self-identity.
Suffering is only a dream
that has been dreamt by your illusionary self.
Become still inside,
and you will feel the radiant light
you have always been and will always be.

Stand alone and unadorned
at the entrance to the temple.
When you are willing to be unencumbered,
the Divine will make you an instrument of eternal grace.

"The person who stands alone will be with the Eloheim; the person who is with the Eloheim will stand alone."

Gospel of Thomas

In the mind of light,
stillness is a natural state.
In the heart of light,
stillness is a place of deep peace.
Stillness is the way to God.

"Let silence speak to you about
the secrets of the universe."

Rumi

To ask the question, "Who am I?"
is the most vital of inquiries.
This inquiry awakens you to your Sacred Source,
which is the truth of your Divine being.

In prayer, the self softens
and the soul becomes the fertile ground
for the flowering of the Beloved.

The disciples said to Jeshua,
"Tell us what Heaven's Kingdom is like."
He said to them,
"It's like a mustard seed,
the smallest of all seeds,
but when it falls on prepared soil,
it produces a large plant
and becomes a shelter for birds of the sky."

Mark 4:31

Witness

God is in your Heart of Light.
Self-realization is turning within and
seeing you are One with the Divine.

Miriam of Magdala

Seeing the Truth

Your eyes of understanding are God's eyes,
but without the judgment of the small self.
Seeing the truth is seeing past the illusionary nature of life
and into the perfection of being.
God is seeing through you when you surrender yourself
into the light of the Divine.
You will then see the true essence of life
without the mistaken identity.

"Meditate within eternity, don't stay in the mind.
Your thoughts are like a child fretting near its
mother's breast, restless and afraid.
With a little guidance, you can
find the path to courage."

Lalla

Be still, and know you are Divine.
See the truth of your life without conditioning.
In truth, there is only pure consciousness.
Breathing deeply, you release all thought
that obstructs your true nature.
Love what is remaining
when the mind is freed from thought.
In your freedom, you will see the truth of being.

Life is a story that holds
both sorrow and joy.

You will not suffer if you become a witness
to your changing story.
On the path of awakening,
you become the seer, not the experience.
You will then be able to rest in the eternal nature of being.

The understanding that we have lost our way
due to our self-importance is critical in order for
us to return to our Divine home of peace.
When we open our heart to Holy wisdom,
the grace of awakening is
ignited within our being.

You are not your body, you are not your mind,
you are not your emotions.
Although, you may experience these veils
of existence with some certainty,
they are only lessons in duality.
These teachings will ultimately lead you home,
to a state of Oneness beyond all
experiences and concepts of self,
to that which we call God.

The Dream

Know yourself as the witness of your life,
and then choose how to dream.
Dream your life into Being.
The manifested world is in duality,
so there will be pleasure and pain,
but the dream is your reality.
The dream is your soul's potential in blossom.

Rest in Spirit, and let go of the
sorrow of the world.
True service is becoming a child
of God and living in your heart
of Sacred love.

In this moment, receive the gifts of Spirit,
an everlasting and untouched beauty, light,
and joy—your eternal blessing.

"I and the Beloved are One."

Jeshua

Jeshua said:
"He who seeks should not stop seeking
until he finds; and when he finds,
he will be bewildered (beside himself);
and when he is bewildered he will marvel,
and will reign over the All."

Gospel of Thomas

Remembering

The calling of your soul
to return to its Divine Home is Master's Grace.

Miriam of Magdala

Living Your Truth

For one to live truth,
their truth needs to start new each day.
Time is the vehicle to awaken to what is true.
The joy of being then becomes your guiding light,
opening your heart to living your truth.
Cherish moments each day to empty your mind,
and rest in the truth of your eternal being.

"He who perceives Me everywhere, and
beholds everything in Me never loses sight
of Me, nor do I ever lose sight of him."

Bhagavad Gita

With each new day, you begin anew.
With each breath, you are breathed by Spirit.
It is most joyous to live the truth of your being.
Breathing in is a miracle of life,
breathing out is your unity with God.
Eternal life is your soul's rest in Divine love.

"Believe in a Love that is being stored up for
you like an inheritance, and have faith that in
this Love there is a strength and a blessing
so large that you can travel as far as you wish
without having to step outside it."

Rainer Maria Rilke

The most important healing is
remembering who you are.
Divine action is to let go of the mind
rooted in the illusion of separation.

Living a Sacred life
is living in Love with the Divine.

Mirror His grace in your life just as
the water reflects the sun's light.

"Come, come, whoever you are.
Wanderer, worshiper, lover of leaving, it doesn't matter.
Ours is not a caravan of despair.
Come, even if you have broken your vow a thousand times.
Come, yet again, come, come."

Rumi

He who perceives Me everywhere
and beholds everything in Me,
never loses sight of Me,
nor do I ever lose sight of him.

BG. VI.30.

Wisdom is knowing
the truth of your
being, devotion is
remembering the
work of your
Sacred heart,
and love is living
for the benefit of all.

Goodness, often buried under sorrow,
is the foundation of all souls.
Through surrender, it is possible to uncover the innate
goodness that lives untouched in the Sacred heart of love.

Light is obstructed in the mind
that is lost in self-identification.
It is through the awakening of Sacred love
that the mind surrenders to the Divine heart.

In times of awakening, your heart breaks open,
becoming a greater vessel of the
Divine love and light;
this is a most Sacred opening.

Light is the force of transformation.
Invoke the light to heal and restore your life to Divinity.

Death is only a second away.
In this life, you move from birth to
death in a moment of time.
Each Sacred moment is preparing you to die
and to live within your timeless being.

Tender moments of
meditation will uncover
the light of your being
that is eternally present
when thought is at rest.

Today is a moment of
time in your life
to remember who you are.

When you remember your Sacred Source,
you will naturally surrender all sense of separation.
In your unified being, you will follow the Divine light
through the veils of manifestation into
the heavenly realms of God.

Deep within the majesty of the universe
and the eternity of time,
we remain but a flicker of light,
while our inner being illuminates all time and space.

Live in the world, but lightly put your feet down,
as if you are walking on clouds.
Heaven is your destination, and Sacred love
will bring you all that you need
for your journey home.

Sacred love awakens the truth in your mind.
This truth becomes your daily practice
for remembering who you are.

Abide in Love.
Allow this Sacred love
to empty you so that
you may become an
instrument of the Divine,
the beginning of true service.

The Sacred temple
of the heart
is where you meet
your mystical Source.
The door to your
inner temple is
open, and
God is waiting.

Now is the time in your soul's evolution to restore its Divinity.
Through understanding your original essence,
you come to realize you are One with all life.

"Knock, and He'll open the door.
Vanish, and He'll make you shine like the sun.
Fall, and He'll raise you to the heavens.
Become nothing, and He'll turn you into everything."

Rumi

Awakening

Prayer is communion with the Source of your Being,
an understanding that all will be
answered through Divine Will.

Miriam of Magdala

Entering the Temple

Begin the journey to your Sacred heart
by turning your attention to the physical heart.
Breathe deeply, allowing your attention to
drop below your physical heart.
Soon, you will feel a presence that will guide you
to the core of your being.
Rest in your inner temple, and you will find God.

"When there are thoughts, it is distraction:
when there are no thoughts, it is meditation."

Ramana Maharshi

Your inner Sacred heart is the opening
to the infinite realm of God.
Take some precious time each day to become more
familiar with your Divine sanctuary within.
Soon you will discover a presence
that has always been there.
This presence will be your guide
to uncover the wisdom of your soul.

Awakening is the grace of your being.
Ask and you shall receive.
In receiving, you will serve.
In serving, you will live eternally in Sacred love.

You are invited to awaken to the
presence of Divine light
in your Sacred heart.
This light removes the seeds of sorrow
and restores you to wholeness.

Sorrow is a result of living life without
knowing your true self.
Peace is the gift of self-realization discovered
in the Sacred heart of love.

I Am
a Shepherd of Men.

The fire of awakening leads you to
surrender your mistaken identity.
In this surrender, you discover a profound freedom of being.
Sacred love is the flame that burns away the roots of sorrow
and uncovers your Divine potential.

.

The Sacred is awakened in your life through the
deep release of the pattern of time and memory.
Through this Divine action, it is possible
to wholly embody every treasured moment.

Drops of sorrow become ripples of movement
in your life as you witness, you are One with the ocean,
your Sacred Source.
You truly realize that your essence is the vastness
of the ocean, and the droplets of sorrow
are the exquisite ripples of change.

The physical body is a portal to
ascend to the light of God.
Your temple is blessed with the breath of Spirit,
a Sacred gift and your birthright.

"Light and darkness,
life and death, right and left,
are brothers of one another.
They are inseparable.
Because of this neither are the
good, nor evil, nor is life, nor death.
For this reason each one will
dissolve into its earliest origin.
But, those who are exalted above
the world are indissoluble, eternal."

Gospel of Phillip

Jeshua said:
"If those who lead you say to you,
See, the Kingdom is in heaven,
then the birds of heaven will go before you.
If they say to you, It is in the sea,
then the fish will go before you.
But the Kingdom is within you,
and it is outside of you."

Gospel of Thomas

Light

Soul healing is letting go of the past,
and in letting go, your Light Being is awakened.

Miriam of Magdala

The Light is Always Shining

Destiny is to realize your light is always shining.
In times of darkness, turn within,
and ask for the light to heal your sorrow.
In times of joy, ask for your light to be used in service.
The Sacred light of your being is always present.

"All sorrows are destroyed upon attainment of tranquility.
The intellect of such a tranquil person soon
becomes completely steady."

Bhagavad Gita

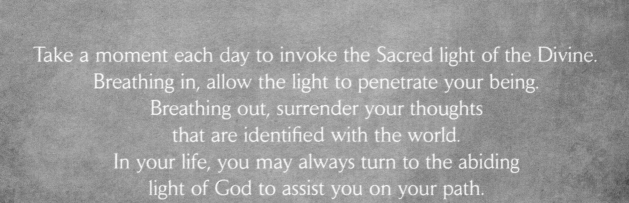

Take a moment each day to invoke the Sacred light of the Divine.
Breathing in, allow the light to penetrate your being.
Breathing out, surrender your thoughts
that are identified with the world.
In your life, you may always turn to the abiding
light of God to assist you on your path.

Trust in My Light,
for you will soon realize it is your Light.

The mind is light when truth originates in the Sacred heart.
An empty mind is a vessel of light.

The light of Divine consciousness
will dissolve the mind in separation.
The love of Divine consciousness
is your path of surrender.
The Sacred Code of Love
is the way of God.

Truth will guide you.
Sacred love will carry you.
The Holy presence will always walk with you.
Leave your burdens behind, and the
light will become your vehicle to
the Kingdom of the Divine.

Service is the key for self-healing.
Service is the pathway to the consciousness of God.
In service, the mind stops self-importance and
becomes devoted to the welfare of others.
Healing occurs when the mind dissolves self-identification.
Serving the goodness of God is the highest work that can be done.
The accumulated ignorance of life is erased when self-importance
ceases to exist. Start now, as this precious birth is temporary.
It will be over in a moment of time.
This life is ultimately for the return to the consciousness of God.

"Be afraid of nothing,
hating none, giving Love to all,
feeling the Love of God,
seeing His presence in everyone,
and having but one desire:
for His constant presence in the
Temple of your Consciousness.
That is the way to live in this world."

Paramahansa Yogananda

Wellspring

The Sacred Code of Love
is your map to freedom and joy.

Miriam of Magdala

Your Eternal Source

God, your eternal Source, will always be with you.
Your Source is the ever-flowing chalice of Divine love
realized in your Sacred heart.
Remember to request all the Divine assistance
you need for your life's journey.

"To understand the immeasurable,
the mind must be extraordinarily quiet, still."

Jiddu Krishnamurti

All of nature is nurtured by one Source.
Open your being to receive the
love and light needed for your life.
The Source of your being will fill your heart
with Divine love by simply asking.
Take time each day to pray to your Source,
giving gratitude for all that you have
and all that will come to be.

Sacred love is your heart of
compassion, where you realize
the profound Oneness
in all of life.

"My soul is a mirror that reveals secrets,
I may not speak about them
but cannot deny knowing.
I run away from body and
soul where I belong,
I swear, I do not know, Seeker,
if you want to know the secret,
first you must die to yourself.
You may see me, but do not think I am here,
I have vanished into my Beloved,
Graced by the essence of love.
My arched back is the bow and my words,
the unbending arrows aimed at Truth.
My tears are testimony of my devotion to
Beloved and from those tears white
lilies will grow that will speak the Truth."

Rumi

"I am the vine, ye are the branches: He that abideth in me, and I in him, the same bringeth forth much fruit: for without me you can do nothing."
John 15:5

In your origin,
in your beginning,
in your wellspring,
lies the truth of your being.
Seek only your Source, and
you will receive the infinite
blessings of the Holy Spirit.

The flowering of your Sacred heart
is unfolding in the beauty
and joy of the Divine.
It is the Source for renewal for
your body, mind, and Spirit.

In your breath lies your
embodied communion with life.
On your inhale and exhale,
Spirit breathes through you.
In this simple exchange with your
Sacred Source lies the gift of
awakening in each moment,
the gift of this precious life.

Sacred love is a never-ending wellspring of the Divine.
Life is a most precious opportunity to live in
Sacred love and to serve the light of the goodness.

The force of Sacred love will guide you to your Divine Source.
Through Oneness with your origin,
your life will be guided and fulfilled.

The longing in your heart for the Divine
is the seed of Sacred love.

I Am the Wellspring that is eternally flowing in Sacred Love.

The human heart has broken into tiny bits of self
from the sorrow of belief in separation.
The invitation is to transform your human heart into your
Sacred heart through opening to the Divine Source.

Life is a difficult journey.
Within this pilgrimage waits the opportunity to
open your heart to a greater love.
Many have chosen to turn away from this grace.
Spirit holds you through the light and dark
as you travel through the tests of
awakening back to Oneness, your Sacred origin.

Trust in
the Divine light
to illuminate
your life path
and guide
you home.

"May today there be peace within.
May you trust that you are
exactly where you are meant to be.
May you not forget the infinite possibilities
that are born of faith in yourself and others.
May you use the gifts that you have received,
and pass on the love that has been given to you.
May you be content with yourself just the way you are.
Let this knowledge settle into your bones, and allow
your soul the freedom to sing, dance, praise and love.
It is there for each and every one of us."

Saint Terese of Liseaux

Gift of Seeing

God is with you all of your life.
In times of sorrow, you will be held.
In times of joy, you will be inspired.
And in the peace of your Being, you will serve.

Miriam of Magdala

Witnessing the Divine

The witness of your true nature sees only God
as the truth of life.
In your light body, the inner eye is awakened,
and the Sacred heart is opened.
The nature of your light body
is the same as God's energy,
only truth is seen, and only love is expressed.

"The mind can go in a thousand directions,
but on this beautiful path, I walk in peace.
With each step, the wind blows.
With each step, a flower blooms."

Thich Nhat Hanh

Within you, there is a portal to the Kingdom of God.
Breathing out, you dissolve the mind of the world.
Breathing in, you journey deep into
the cavern of your heart, opening the door
to your inner Kingdom.
It is here that you realize the truth of your being,
and you become the witness of your life.

God is the
all-pervading eye
that sees through
your eyes.
Love is the seeing of
another as Divine,
a mirror of God.
This is true service.

When you see another soul's light,
they begin to realize their own light.
Most souls are rarely seen for the light
inside their being. Often, they are seen
through the eyes of the mind
instead of through the light of the heart.
Many souls are suffering from
not being truly seen.
To mirror the light of
another is an act of Sacred love.
The honoring of truth in all
living things, is a cherished gift.

"There are
So many positions of Love:

Each curve on a branch,

The thousand different ways
Your eyes can embrace us,

The infinite shapes your
Mind can draw,

The spring
Orchestra of scents,

The currents of light combusting
Like passionate lips,

The revolution of Existence's skirt
Whose folds contain other worlds.

Your every sigh that falls against
His inconceivable
Omnipresent Body."

Hafiz

"That inner Self, as the primeval Spirit,
Eternal, ever effulgent, full and infinite Bliss,
Single, indivisible, whole and living,
shines in everyone as the witnessing awareness.
That self in its splendour, shining in the cavity of the heart.
This self is neither born nor dies,
Neither grows nor decays,
Nor does it suffer any change.
When a pot is broken,
the space within it is not,
And similarly, when the body dies,
the Self in it remains eternal."
Sri Ramana Maharshi

Sacred love is your heart of compassion.
Where you realize the profound
Oneness in all of life.

I Am
One with Nature.

Life expressed in nature
has no thought of Self.

The disciples said to Jeshua,
"Tell us how our end will be."
Jeshua said,
"Have you discovered, then, the beginning,
that you look for the end?
For where the beginning is, there will the end be.
Blessed is he who will take his place in the beginning;
he will know the end and will not experience death."

Gospel of Thomas

Master's Grace

The Sacred Code of Love is
Master's Wisdom in your heart.
Listen within to receive guidance for your life.

Miriam of Magdala

Rest in My Grace

Grace of being is unity of God and self.
The Divine is always guiding you home to grace.
Trust in your path of awakening,
and rest in the arms of your Beloved inner teacher;
then you will know grace.
Your Sacred heart is the temple of grace for you
to rest and rejuvenate your soul.

"We contemplate that reality in which everything exists,
to which everything belongs,
from which everything has emerged,
which is the cause of everything,
and which is everything."

Sage Vasishtha

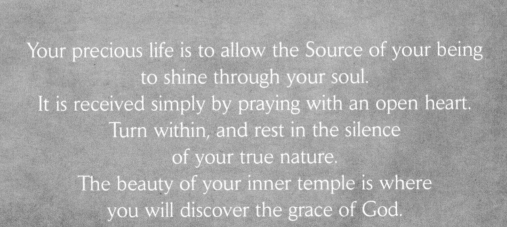

Your precious life is to allow the Source of your being
to shine through your soul.
It is received simply by praying with an open heart.
Turn within, and rest in the silence
of your true nature.
The beauty of your inner temple is where
you will discover the grace of God.

Live in the
heart of God,
and disappear from
the worldly pursuit.
Let your soul
climb the
stairway to Heaven.

"I traveled a long way
seeking God, but when I finally
gave up and turned back,
there He was, inside of me."
Lalla

The grace of God is in your life at all times.
In times of sorrow, grace opens your Sacred heart
to receive more light.
In times of joy, you realize
that grace has been with you along.

Meditate within your Sacred heart,
and you will know grace.

The temple of your Sacred heart is where we meet.
Now, the door is open to become One with the Divine.
Come to the altar of the Divine, and restore your life
to beauty, joy, and peace.

God's grace lives through you
as you discover you are an
empty vessel for the Divine.

"If you bring forth what is within you,
what you bring forth will save you.
If you do not bring forth what is within you,
what you do not bring forth will destroy you."
Gospel of Thomas

I Am
the Light of your heart.

I Am
the Love of your heart.

I Am
the Light of the World.

God is always with you in your eternal being.
When the body dies, your soul lives on
eternally in your light body.
The Sacred Code of Love, when activated in your Sacred heart,
will strengthen your light body so it may
journey to higher realms of consciousness.
The Sacred Code of Love is awakened through periods of
deep silence and communion with your Divine Source.

"If you say that the abode of the Gods is in the sky,
the birds will arrive there before you.
If you say it is in the sea,
the fish will arrive there before you.
Know that the heavenly realm is both
inside you and outside you,
and you will know that which is outside
by that which is inside.
When you have found the Light within yourselves,
you will know as you are known."

Gospel of Thomas

Open Your Heart and Receive Our Love

The transmission of grace occurs in silence of being.
This is your Holy time of communion with
the light and love of God.
Remember that grace is always with you
throughout your journey in your precious life.

"This is what should be done
By one who is skilled in goodness,
And who knows the path of peace:
Let them be able and upright,
Straightforward and gentle in speech.
Humble and not conceited,
Contented and easily satisfied.
Unburdened with duties
and frugal in their ways.
Peaceful and calm, and wise and skillful,
Not proud and demanding in nature.
Let them not do the slightest thing
That the wise would later reprove.
Wishing: In gladness and in safety,
May all beings be at ease.
Whatever living beings there may be;
Whether they are weak
or strong, omitting none,
The great or the mighty, medium,
short or small,
The seen and the unseen,
Those living near and far away,
Those born and to-be-born,
May all beings be at ease!

Let none deceive another,
Or despise any being in any state.
Let none through anger or ill-will
Wish harm upon another.
Even as a mother protects with her life
Her child, her only child,
So with a boundless heart
Should one cherish all living beings:
Radiating kindness over the entire world
Spreading upwards to the skies,
And downwards to the depths;
Outwards and unbounded,
Freed from hatred and ill-will.
Whether standing or walking,
seated or lying down
Free from drowsiness,
One should sustain this recollection.
This is said to be the sublime abiding.
By not holding to fixed views,
The pure-hearted one,
having clarity of vision,
Being freed from all sense desires,
Is not born again into this world."

Buddha, Metta Sutta

His disciples said,
"Show us the place where you are, for we must seek it."
He said to them, "Anyone here with two ears had better listen!
There is light within a person of light, and it shines on
the whole world. If it does not shine, it is dark."
Gospel of Thomas

I Am
the Bread of Life.

"Ask, and it will be given to you;
seek, and you will find;
knock, and it will be
opened to you.
For everyone who asks receives,
and he who seeks finds,
and to him who knocks
it will be opened."

Mathew 7:7

Miriam and Jeshua's Prayer

Our teachers, the guiding Light of the
Divine, hallowed be your names.
We pray that you will eternally guide us
so we may Unify with the
Love and Light of the Divine.
Within our Sacred Heart,
we enter the Kingdom,
where we receive your Grace.
Forgive us for our separation and our
trespasses against one another,
and lead us to greater and deeper
devotion, as it is in your Light we serve.
For God is the Kingdom, and the Power,
and Glory for Eternal Life.
Amen

Jaya Sarada—Message Receiver and Teacher

Jewels, also known as Jaya Sarada, began walking the path of truth many years ago. Growing up in Ojai, California, Jewels learned about truth through beauty, nature, and the transmission of silence.

Her mother Marjorie Keller was a seeker on the path of awakening and spent most of her life learning from teachers, living and traveling throughout India, and inquiring into the nature of true reality. Her mother's husband Dr. Keller was the personal physician to J. Krishnamurti. Through a deep study of Krishnamurti's teachings and Theosophy, Marjorie blessed the family with a strong spiritual foundation. Jewels has spent many years studying spiritual teachings and learning from her awakened mother. Jewels, being guided to return to her true nature, went through the trials of separation from her Sacred Source, the sorrow of forgetfulness, and the pain of not knowing true, Divine love.

While exploring India, the seed of truth within Jewels began to blossom. The path of awakening for Jewels has brought her to her knees throughout her life, as she learned to surrender the false nature of the self, opening her heart to a greater love and devotion to the Divine. Through Divine guidance, Jewels became aware of her Sacred family of origin. The presence of Jeshua and Miriam and other great Beings of Light appeared in her life. Through quiet communion with the Holy Forces that overshadowed her life, she began receiving and writing down the messages of **The Sacred Code of Love,** which she now graciously shares with you, dear reader.

Arielle Beauduy—Transcriber and Assistant Editor

Arielle Beauduy is the transcriber of the messages received in *The Sacred Code of Love* book. Through the experience of these profound messages, she has found her path and offering of service. It is an honor for Arielle to work beside her mother and it is with deep reverence that they offer this Sacred work to the world.

It is Arielle's mission, that through the teachings of *Jeshua, Miriam* and *The Sacred Council of Light™,* the beings on this planet are re-set in the frequency of light and love; their birthright.

Arielle is also a facilitator of gatherings and the Director of *The Magdalene Sisterhood™* as well as the Assistant Director of *The Sacred Council of Light™*. In the gatherings, Arielle interweaves her unique movement offering called *ConsciousMotion™*. Her movement style is a blend of yoga, energy clearing techniques and organic transitions, which is aimed at bringing forth ease, vitality and freedom of being through mindful movement practices. A key aspect of her work now is called *Zero Point Clearing*, which is an experience aimed at re-setting the frequency of the body, mind, Spirit trinity, so the Sacred heart can be fully experienced in the present. Her work also focuses on communion with Spirit through joyful expression and the experience of light, love, grace and beauty in communal settings.

Arielle's message is;
"as we awaken the light within,
the world resonates with more light,
grace fills our daily lives and we
become whole in the love of serving God."

Arielle Beauduy's website
www.consciousmotion.com.

Life, A Pause
Let the fullness embody you
Nothing to remove, Nothing to gain
A Presence floods your perception
Seeing remains in the
mystery of no-mind
Through effort you forget
Through hearing with the breath
of Spirit, you remember

– Arielle Beauduy

The Sacred Code of Love *Worldwide Events*

The Flowering of the Sacred Heart
Workshop

The practice of the **Flowering of The Sacred Heart**, offers the discovery of your inherent unity with God, which is the very Source of your being. Experience a Holy devotion to tmoruth, which naturally dissolves harmful perceptions which limit your capacity as an expressive being of Divine love. Through these 5 spiritual practices; Prayer, Presence, Release, Transcendence, and Rest, you will be guided on the passageway through your Sacred heart, and will experience your timeless radiant essence. The altar of the Divine lives within your heart, an eternal temple in which you may recede and rest, and offer any suffering that is held in your field to the compassionate caretaker of your soul. Join us as Spiritual beings, who are in reverence of this human experience, as we reach together for our Divine potential.

In this workshop we will explore and receive guidance on the following 5 practices:

- **Prayer:** Use the *Intention of God* to hold the frequency of the Divine. You are a Holy temple of light. **The *Intention of God* allows what is false to simply drop away, and what is revealed is the presence of unified God consciousness.**

- **Presence:** In *Presence,* you will realize you are a container for your life experience, you are not the content, only the seer. It is through this very witnessing, that your life is transformed. **In *Presence*, You are That which Is.**

- **Release**: Breath-Out. Upon the altar of your Sacred heart, you may surrender all that is not of service to your Divine being and expression. Reset to your timeless and formless essence. **In *letting-go*, you commune with God.**

- **Transcendence**. Breath-In. Experience the wholeness of your being, receive the gift of love and light. **The *Transcendence* of that which is false, is the opening of your Sacred heart.**

- **Rest:** Simply rest in the grace and peace of being. The actualization, the embodiment of your Sacred heart. **Rest in the gentle embrace of your eternal Beloved.**

The blessings of your Sacred heart are here now, just a precious breath away.

Grace of Being
Satsang *"A Gathering of Truth"*

Come as you are, where-ever you are in your life, you are welcome here. We stand at the beginning to return to our origin. In this returning we are gifted with presence of being, now, without a past, without a future. In timeless presence, we are guided by The Sacred Council of Light to activate the lost memory of our true nature, to align our energy fields with our diamond potential, and to step into a life of sincere service to that which is eternal, unified, luminous and infused with the pure devotional love. You are invited to attend Satsang, *A Gathering of Truth.*

Grace of Being Satsang is an invitation to enter the silence space of your being.

Communion with Love
A Gathering with The Magdalene Sisterhood

The Expression of the Beloved Feminine in Spirit

Joy ∽ Grace ∽ Beauty ∽ Love ∽ Light!

The Magdalene Sisterhood offers the kinship of the Divine Feminine in all beings from all backgrounds, races, ethnicities, orientations and religions. Our gatherings are an experience in the grace, joy, love, beauty and light that we all share, through our very essence as spiritual beings. A devotional, supportive and joyfully expressive gathering of the Sacred!

Event Booking and Registration:
Our events are healing, elevating, supportive and help build strong positive spiritual connections in our dear community. We would love to hold an event near you!

To book *The Sacred Code of Love* event at your venue, please email:
 info@sacredcodeoflove.com or call toll free 1-855-505-3935.

To register for an event, please visit our gathering page at:
 www.thesacredcodeoflove.com or call toll free 1-855-505-3935.

Blessings
The Light in Me, Honors and Sees the Light in You

Dear Readers,

We hope you have enjoyed reading **The Sacred Code of Love.**

If you would like to be on our mailing list to learn about upcoming workshops, events, and our nationwide tour, please join our mailing list at www.thesacredcodeoflove.com or call our toll free number at 1.855.505.3935.

Visit www.thesacredcodeoflove for a FREE MP3 download sample of
The Sacred Code of Love CD.

TO ORDER **The Sacred Code of Love CD**
produced by Charlie Braun
with recited passages to flute, crystsl bowls,
guitar and kirtan, contact us at:

info@thesacredcodeoflove.com

CPSIA information can be obtained at www.ICGtesting.com
Printed in the USA
BVOW10s2014240315

393172BV00004B/4/P